IMAGES
of England

AROUND
PULBOROUGH

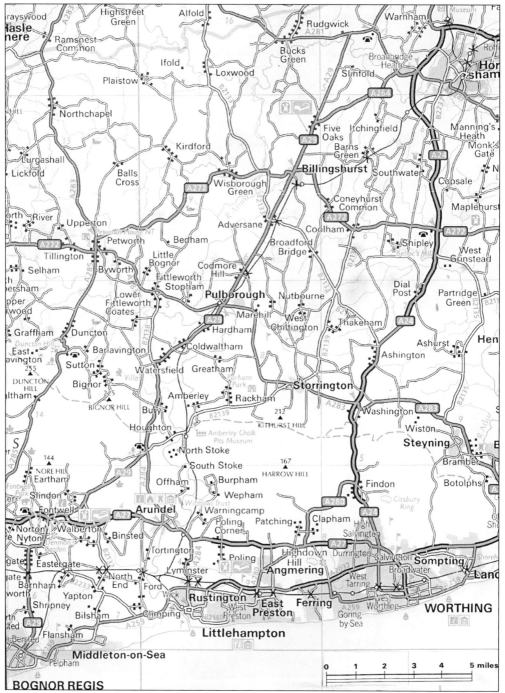

Pulborough is strategically situated at the junction of the A29 and the A272. Stane Street, which was the Roman road from Chichester to London, can be seen as part of the straight line running from the village to beyond Billingshurst.

IMAGES
of England

AROUND
PULBOROUGH

P.A.L. Vine

TEMPUS

First published 2002
Copyright © P.A.L. Vine, 2002

Tempus Publishing Limited
The Mill, Brimscombe Port,
Stroud, Gloucestershire, GL5 2QG

ISBN 0 7524 2611 7

Typesetting and origination by
Tempus Publishing Limited
Printed in Great Britain by
Midway Colour Print, Wiltshire

Cover illustration: Clements Bridge, 1895. An artistic representation from a postcard (see p. 88).

Fifty years ago visitors would send this postcard to their friends. The saddler's shop (top left) at the bottom of Church Hill is now a private residence, the boat-house by Stopham Bridge was swept away in the great flood in 1968, but both the church with its famous lych gate and the old bridge remain.

4

Contents

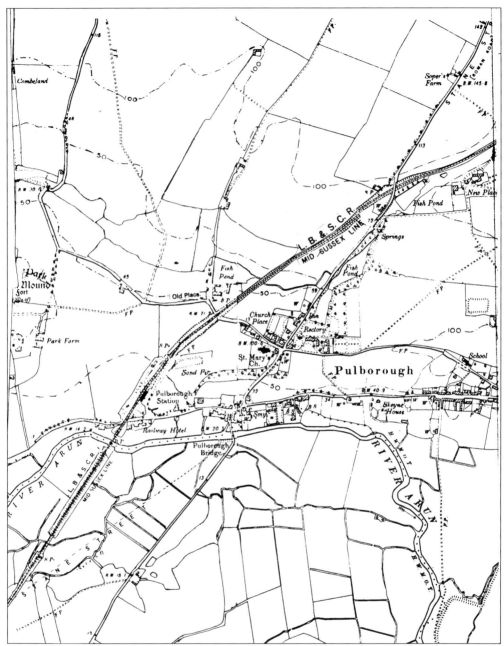

The six-inch ordnance map of 1914 shows Pulborough as it appeared before the First World War. Pulborough Bridge was known as Swan Bridge. Old Place, New Place, the Railway Hotel and the rectory (whose extensive grounds and fish ponds are no more) are clearly marked.

Introduction

Pulborough is a long straggling village situated on the banks of the River Arun in the south-west corner of an extensive parish of over 6,000 acres. The main street is Lower Street where houses still hug the roadway as they have done for centuries in spite of attempts to widen the thoroughfare where cottages have been demolished. Indeed one of the phenomenons of recent years has been the way country villages have changed so much in character. Road improvements, car parks, the increase in council housing, the development of industrial estates, the conversion of farm workers' cottages and the closure of public houses and village shops have all produced changes which have occurred since I came to live in Pulborough 40 years ago.

During the nineteenth century there was little fluctuation in the size of the population. In 1831 it was 1,979 and was still only 2,065 a century later. However the electrification of the railway line to London in 1936 brought the first regular commuters travelling to the City but even so, numbers had only risen to 2,474 by 1951. Every 10 years the increase gathered pace by 385, then 507 and 767 in 1981. By 1991 the number had grown to 4,240 and in the last decade's census it is estimated to be nearly 5,000.

Until the early part of the twentieth century there were no street pavements, nor lamps, and road drainage, where it existed, was an open gutter bridged by flagstones. Until 1910 houses had to rely on wells for their water supply and used garden privies for their personal needs. Aladdin lamps and candles were in regular demand. However main drainage was introduced in 1959, a new library was opened in 1966 and Sainsbury's supermarket in 2000. But none of these events would have changed village life as much as what could have happened in 1827 when a giant ship canal, the width of a motorway and 28 ft deep, was planned to pass through the parish. The Grand Imperial Ship Canal was intended to take the largest ships from the Thames to Portsmouth. Although a bill was presented to Parliament in February 1828, John Rennie condemned the project on the grounds of natural difficulty and enormous expense.

However the past 50 years have seen a considerable change in the nature of the village. The Swan Hotel and the old Railway hotel have been demolished and the Arun Hotel converted into flats. Georgian and Victorian houses with their extensive gardens have been likewise divided and sub-divided. Cottages and Edwardian villas have been flattened to make way for new dwellings. The introduction of Value Added Tax has ensured spiralling costs for repairs and services for every domestic need. No longer are there in the village a bakery, saddler, shoe repairer, tobacconist or teashop. The railway station no longer has a porter so elderly people have a more difficult time getting their baggage down and up the steep flight of steps when catching the London train. On the other side of the coin we have mini-supermarkets, a Chinese takeaway, a ladies' hairdresser and a betting shop.

Nevertheless many fine buildings remain and this book sets out to record not only what has been destroyed but also what remains to be admired. The countryside, the South Downs and the river remain as lovely as ever.

P.A.L Vine
January 2002

MESSRS. CROSS and Co. impressed with the deepest sense of obligation for the kind and flattering interest which has been manifested in their favour since they established their

ELEGANT AND COMMODIOUS COACH

The Comet,

BY THE SHORTEST AND MOST PLEASANT ROAD

TO ARUNDEL,
LITTLE HAMPTON
and Bognor,

Through LEATHERHEAD, DORKING, OCKLEY, BILLINGSHURST and PULBOROUGH,

beg leave most respectfully to announce, that it has determined them to run another Coach, so as to afford a daily communnication to and from the Metropolis.

THESE COACHES LEAVE THE

Ship Tavern,

CHARING CROSS, LONDON,

AND THE BEACH HOTEL, LITTLE HAMPTON,

EVERY MORNING AT SEVEN o'CLOCK;

The NEW INN, BOGNOR at a Quarter *Before* SEVEN,

And the Norfolk Arms, Arundel,

AT EIGHT;

and they flatter themselves that their desire to contribute to the comfort, safety, and convenience of the Public, will entitle them to a further claim on the liberality of the Public.
Calls at the George and Gate, Gracechurch Street, and the Bell and Crown Inn, Holborn.
Messrs. CROSS and Co. pledge themselves their Coaches shall arrive in Town punctually at Five o'Clock.
Langley, Typ.

Every morning in the 1830s *The Comet* passed through the village on its way from Littlehampton to Charing Cross. Not until after the opening of Pulborough station in 1859 did the local coach services cease.

One
Swan Bridge

This view of Swan Bridge painted in 1891 shows at centre left the entrance to the cut from the river that allowed barges to unload grain for the Corn Exchange. There was also a dock on the left bank just above the bridge where barges could be repaired at low water. In the 1830s the Arundel Lighter Company's boats passed by daily to convey goods between London, Arundel and Chichester.

Swan Bridge and Harry Fielder's cottage from an old watercolour, *c.* 1850.

The decision to build a new bridge spelt the end of Fielder's Cottage whose south wall can just be distinguished behind the paraphernalia of the building contractors in 1934. (Garland)

The new bridge under construction looking south in 1935 six months after work had begun. (Garland)

Fielder's Cottage stood in the middle of the highway between the Swan Hotel and Arun House. Here Fielder ran a greengrocer's and fishmonger's shop outside which were displayed bouquets of flowers and trays of fruit and vegetables.

Pulborough Wharf, *c.* 1920. The barge repair dock can be seen at left centre next to George Floate's hut from which he and his family let punts and skiffs until the late 1950s.

St Mary's church can be seen in the background.

PULBOROUGH, SUSSEX.

TO be SOLD by PRIVATE CONTRACT.—

That old Established Commercial and Posting House THE SWAN INN, of Pulborough, together with a Meadow and walled-in Garden, connected with the same.—This is the only Commercial and Posting House in the place, and is now in full trade.—A better opportunity for investment or laying out of property in rate cannot be offered.—The House is at present in the occupation of Mr. J. Trower, whose Lease will expire at Lady-day, 1833, when possession may be had by taking off the Stock in Trade, &c. of the present tenant, at a fair valuation.—This House is situated well for business, as it stands on the cross-roads from London to Arundel, Little Hampton, Bognor, and the Brighton Road, to the Western parts of England; Coaches each road daily. The Corn Market is held weekly at this Inn, in a large Assembly-room, which will contain 300 persons.—It has accommodation for 100 horses; also Coach-house, Granary, &c —The situation of this House is most healthy, as it is near the banks of the river Arun; it communicates with the sea at Little Hampton; by Canal from Portsmouth to London three times a-week.—For further particulars apply to Mr. Francis Jarrett, Pulborough.—If by letter, post-paid.

N.B.—The Premises are Freehold.

Advertisement from the *Hampshire Telegraph*, 13 August 1832. By the turn of the nineteenth century the Swan had become an important posting house with stabling for forty horses, as two additional horses were required to assist the mail coaches to climb Church Hill. The reference in the advertisement to accommodate 100 horses was rather exaggerated!

The back of the Swan Hotel as it appeared in 1902. William Jennings became landlord of the Swan in the early 1890s and remained there for over fifty years. He also became the proprietor of the Corn Exchange and in 1912 the Swan was advertised as being the headquarters of the Automobile Association offering accommodation for motoring parties and fishermen.

Mr and Mrs Jennings preparing to set off with their friends in their carriage and four for the Goodwood races, c. 1900.

Swan Bridge, 1930. The bridge was built in 1785 with three arches, with a fourth arch added in 1834.

A 1991 view of the rebuilt 'Swan' after it had reverted to being a pub and a restaurant. It is a sign of the times that both were closed in 2001 and that the site is now being developed for more housing. At right can be seen the former granary, now converted into offices. The awning next to the granary shielded the window of the newsagent and tobacconist and this too closed for want of business in 1999.

Two
The River Arun

The view of the tidal river looking downstream from Swan Bridge in the early 1950s. The Arun is the longest river in Sussex. It rises in St Leonard's Forest near Horsham, and according to the 1877 report of a House of Lords Committee on Conservancy Boards, it flows $51\frac{1}{2}$ miles to the English Channel at Littlehampton. The lower reaches have been used for moving goods and chattels since the Norman Conquest and the river was made navigable as far as Stopham Bridge during the reign of Queen Elizabeth I.

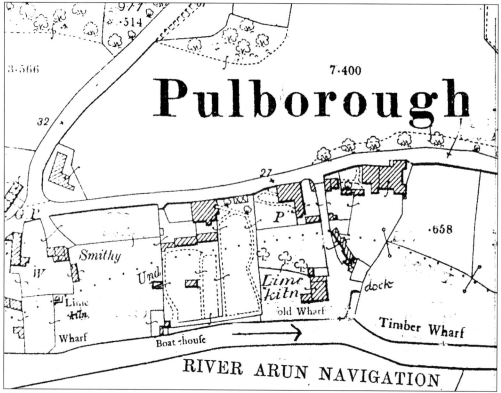

The riverbank at Pulborough in 1876. The straightening of the River Arun during the second half of the sixteenth century caused wharves to be established along the north bank and limekilns to be built. The dotted line on the map indicates the former course of the river before it was diverted. The dock by the limekiln depicted on the 1851 tithe map was last used in the 1870s. The wharf marked below the Smithy was known as Puddle Wharf.

A 1930s view of the ramshackle collection of corrugated iron sheds below the bridge, which had formerly been used as storehouses for the river trade.

The wooden boathouse at Templemead, photographed in 1921, which survived the floods until 1940.

The appearance of the navigation around Pulborough in the early 1840s is reflected in the charming line drawings by Thomas Evershed. Evershed's father was a yeoman farmer who married Mary Martin, the daughter of Dr P.P. Martin, the owner of Templemead, Pulborough. Thomas, the second of a family of nine children, was born at Pallingham Farm in 1817. In 1822 his father went to America to buy land, but while his wife and family were travelling to join him, he died. Mrs Evershed stayed long enough to sell the farm he had bought and returned to England in 1836 leaving Thomas and their elder son in America. Seven years later Thomas, while visiting his mother, rode round the neighbourhood sketching her favourite views.

This pedestal was erected by Dr Martin in memory of Charles James Fox (1749-1806), former MP for Midhurst and then Westminster and later Secretary of State for Foreign Affairs, who used to play chess on a board set in the floor of the temple. The sides of the pedestal were inscribed to celebrate the abolition of slavery in the British Commonwealth, and is seen around 1920. It was Fox who had moved the motion for the abolition only a few days before his death.

Dr Peter Patrick Martin aged sixty. He bought Templemead in 1789 and built the garden temple in 1793. He was the father of nine children and after retiring from his medical practice in 1833, was succeeded by his son Dr Peter John Martin (1786-1860) who was also distinguished as a geologist, and a frequent contributor to *The Gardeners Chronicle*.

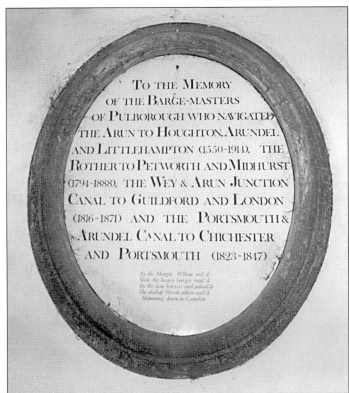

To the Memory
of the Barge-masters
of Pulborough who navigated
the Arun to Houghton, Arundel
and Littlehampton (1550-1914), the
Rother to Petworth and Midhurst
(1794-1888), the Wey & Arun Junction
Canal to Guildford and London
(1816-1871) and the Portsmouth &
Arundel Canal to Chichester
and Portsmouth (1823-1847)

By the Margin, Willow veil'd
Slide the heavy barges trail'd
By the slow horses; and unhail'd
The shallop flitteth silken-sail'd
Skimming down to Camelot

A memorial plaque erected to the barge masters of Pulborough.

Robert Goodsall related how in the early 1950s he came upon a row-boat whose occupants were engaged in cutting reeds and observed the water-pavilion, 'in the form of a Doric portico which stood against a leafy background of tall trees, its columns and pediment lovingly reflected in the flood water'.

Waterside House, formerly Bowler's dairy, seen from the river in 1960. The ruins of the former stone limekiln can be seen behind the poplar tree. In the eighteenth century a wooden bridge here provided access to the water meadows.

The substantial eighteenth-century limekiln on the Old Wharf as seen in the 1930s. The stone limekiln had two furnaces and measured 40ft x 30ft. On the east side was the dock which silted up in the 1870s. A few posts and piles remained in 1953. In June 1789 the Arun Navigation Company leased the Old Wharf from the devisees of Thomas Hampton for ninety-nine years at £6 per year and in December 1804 the company agreed that Thomas Stone should maintain the wharf for the benefit of the bargemen.

A pre-Second World War view of the village of Pulborough. In 1931 the population was only 2,065 but by 1991 it had more than doubled. The meadows are now built over and even the chimney pots at right, which belonged to the Arun Hotel, have vanished.

Number 64 below Pulborough Bridge in 1898 with Barge master Henry Doick and his sons Percy and Tom. In the space of six years (1895–1901) he made 521 voyages up and down the Arun carrying 17,096 tons of cargo between Littlehampton and Pulborough.

Bargemaster Sam Strudwick was one of the last carriers on the Arun Navigation. This view of the *Reliance* was taken in 1913. She was sold to the Arun Brick Company in 1923 and in 1925 the Harbour master at Littlehampton reported that it had been agreed that the abandoned barge should be given to the Commissioners of the Port of Arundel in return for its removal from the tideway.

PULBOROUGH, RIVER ARUN. 30971 JUDGES LTD.

The Arun flowing south towards the English Channel. In the 1960s the river authority removed the sharper sinuousities, cut down the trees and raised clay embankments to reduce flooding but causing, alas, the waterway to lose much of its rural charm.

Three
Church Hill

At the bottom of Church Hill was the saddler's shop. James Albery is listed as the harness maker in 1832. He retired in 1874 to be followed by Peacock, Whitcombe and from 1890 by David Dilloway and later by his widow. James Orfold ran the business for twenty years before it was bought by W. Langham towards the end of the Second World War. By now however, harness work had dwindled and he concentrated on repairing all manner of leather goods including bellows and engraving dog collars. After Langham retired in 1959 the shop became a greengrocer's and then a hairdressing salon before reverting to being a private residence.

Horncroft and Old Timbers are two of the oldest cottages in the village dating back to the fifteenth century. A Tudor chimney was discovered during restoration work forty years ago as well as a bedroom wall made of wattle and daub of straw and manure. Opposite is a wooden-clad building which used to be known as the Coffee Tavern or Reading Room. This was opened in 1882 and was used for meetings of the Men's Club until it was moved to the Church Rooms at the top of the hill in 1906.

Descending Church Hill in summer and, right, a winter during the 1930s when there was an open gutter and no pavement.

Church Hill.

The drawing of the old cottage at the top of Church Hill by Frederick Griggs appeared in the first edition of E.V. Lucas's *Highways & Byways in Sussex* in 1903, but the gnarled tree roots and the shepherd with his flock suggest an earlier date. The cottage was originally built in the fifteenth century on the same level as the churchyard. When the road was lowered in 1757 the substantial brick wall was built to protect the base of the building.

The old cottage at the top of Church Hill as it appeared in 1895. The notice board at left warns cyclists of the dangerous gradient down to Swan Corner. It was not uncommon for them to land somewhat shaken outside the blacksmith's forge at the bottom of the hill.

S.H. Grimm's drawing of St Mary's church from the north east, 1791.

Pulborough Church, Sussex.

The oldest part of the church is the chancel built around 1180 and the nave and aisles were added in the fifteenth century. The church registers date from 1595. There are several brasses, a Norman font, piscina and sedilia of different styles.

The oldest bell in the Bell Tower dates from around 1500.

Verger's Cottage was built in the late 1830s on the site of a house called 'Fustians', which formed part of the Rectory Manor.

St Mary's church with its celebrated lych-gate crowns the hilltop close to where Stane Street, the Roman road passed on its way from Chichester to London. Church Place is an area of special architectural and historic interest with terraced houses of various ages and architectural styles.

Chequers Hotel after the disastrous fire on 15 November 1963. There were no casualties but the seven elderly guests had to make a hurried exit in the early hours of the morning. Firemen from Billingshurst, Petworth and Storrington took nearly five hours to get the fire under control. Only the small chapel at the rear of the garden survived. Chequers Hotel was a sixteenth-century property, which was known in the nineteenth century as the Chequers Inn and Posting House.

Four
Rectory Lane

Chequers Hotel moved to the corner of Rectory Lane in 1963. This was once the site of a seventeenth-century property known as 'Braziers' which belonged to the Rectory Manor. It was sold to a miller in 1628 for £25 and in 1675 to a butcher for £80. In 1866 it had become a draper's and was still a shop in 1939 known as the Church Stores.

The Queen Anne Rectory was built by the Revd Francis Mose, Rector 1718-29. The glebe then exceeded 160 acres. Harvey Spragg, Rector 1767-96, developed six acres of garden which were famous for the variety of exotic trees. During the reign of Queen Victoria a third floor was added but this was removed in 1952 so that the house retained its original appearance until it was converted into flats some years ago.

The Rectory seen here in 1986, much as it would have appeared in 1821, without a second floor.

A fifteenth-century monastery chapel which stands at the rear of the former Chequers Hotel and escaped the fire.

The almshouses by the war memorial were used as homes for retired priests and their wives or widows.

St Mary's Church of England School and the former master's house which was built in 1857. The school building had three classrooms and the common opposite was used as a playground. Central heating and the insertion of new windows came in 1924 but in 1971 the school was closed and the site sold for housing development.

The view from Rectory Meadow looking across the water meadows of the River Arun. It is very much hoped that this glebe land, which still belongs to the church, will remain sacrosanct to change of use.

Five
The London Road

Stane Street, the former Roman road from Chichester to London, passed through the parish. Beyond Church Hill it is now more commonly known as the London Road (A41) where the Five Bells stands to the west before Codmore Hill is reached. Reputed to be the oldest inn in the village, it is recorded that there was a pub here in 1706 but only since 1821 has it been called the Five Bells. Before the First World War the London Road was very narrow with a rough stony surface and only wide enough for a horse and cart. This view shows the inn sign with Charles Medlock's name, the innkeeper from 1905 to 1914. Sadly the inn closed in 2000 and is now boarded up.

In 1987, the new owners of the Five Bells carried out major restoration work during which two wells, a large three-breasted chimney with open fireplace and ancient walls built of flint and stone, and even of wattle and daub were discovered.

The first police station was sited on the Stopham road in the 1840s (see p. 87). In 1936 a new station was built between the church and the railway bridge. This underwent major alterations in 1951 when the cells were abolished. Nowadays it is rare to find a policeman on duty although this recent picture belies the fact!

CODMORE HILL, nr. Pulborough, Sussex. [*Map* 6.*E*.2.] London 45½ miles.

E. Closing—Wed. Post—7.30 p.m.
Billingshurst 4□ Storrington 5½, Pulborough 1□.

GARAGE.

✱   **A. E. Johnson & Sons**; T.A., Johnson, Haulage, Pulborough; T.N. Pulborough 25; G.A.—C. 6; M/C. 8; O.S.

†**PULBOROUGH** (2,065), Sussex. (Goodwood Races.) [*Map* 6.*E*.2.] London 46½ miles.

L.H. 10.30-2.30, 6-10 w.d.; 12-2, 7-10 S. M. Day—Alt. Mon. E. Closing—Wed. Post—7.30 p.m.
Ten Mile Speed Limit.
Codmore Hill 1, Billingshurst 5½, Dorking 23, Horsham 12½□ Storrington 5, Brighton 23½, Worthing 15□ Arundel 9½, Littlehampton 13½, Bognor 16½, Chichester 17□ Petworth 5½, Petersfield 21½□.

HOTELS.

✱   **Railway**, Station Road; T.A., Kitchin; T.N., 9; 5 brms.; R. 4/-; B. 3/-; L.c. 2/6; L.h. 3/- to 3/6; T. 1/3; D. 4/6; G.A.—C.60; f.d.m.; 1/- N.
✱   **Swan**; T.N., 10; 10 brms.; S.R. 4/6 to 5/-; D.R. 7/6 to 8/-; B. 3/-; L.c. daily 3/-; L.h. 3/6; T. 1/3; D. 4/6; Ch. 10/-; G.A.—C. 14; L.u. 6; f.d.m.; 1/- N.

GARAGES.

✱✱✱ **Pulborough Motor Engineering Works** (P. Kitchin), Lower Street and Railway Garage; T.A., Kitchin; T.N., 9; G.A.—C. 20; M/C. 20; O.N. at call (Railway Garage); O.S.; C.h.
✱   **A. E. Johnson & Sons**, Codmore Hill; T.A., Haulage; T.N., 25; G.A.—

In early editions of the AA Handbook Codmore Hill had its own separate entry, as this extract from the 1928 edition shows. Observe that motorists are warned that the speed limit in Pulborough is 10mph.

Stane Street viewed from the crown of Codmore Hill looking towards Billingshurst. In the early twentieth century the locality had several shops, a blacksmith, a wheelwright, a sub-post office (at right) and the Rose & Crown (at left) which was built in the 1870s with a thatched roof. This photograph was taken after it was rebuilt following the fire in 1915.

and also to amend, alter, or heighten any Bridge or Bridges, which may any ways hinder or obstruct the said intended Navigation; and also to get, dig, take, and carry away Soil, Chalk, Clay, Gravel, or Stone, proper, requisite, or convenient, for making, carrying, altering, or continuing the said Works and Undertakings, in or from any Grounds of any Person or Persons adjoining or lying contiguous to the said River, or to or from the Stone Quarry at Cudmore Hill, in the Parish of Pulborough

to alter Bridges,

and dig Chalk, &c. from the adjacent Grounds;

The section of the 1785 Arun Navigation Act which authorized the taking and carrying away of building materials for the canal bridges and locks from the stone quarry at Codmore Hill.

There were several substantial stone quarries on Codmore Hill although none have been worked since the First World War. However one to the west of Hill Farm (marked B on the 1876 Ordnance Survey), is well maintained as a nature reserve on private property.

Six

Old Place and New Place

Old Place, the former estate of the Apsleys, was built in the reign of Henry VI (1422-1461). It enclosed a court and the superstructure was of timber with large square windows, many of which were projecting. This view was taken before reconstruction took place in the 1920s.

Old Place as it appeared in 1974.

Old Place and the fishpond which is famous for its carp.

The Great Hall of Old Place
Manor, 1964.

Drawings of Old Place by A.S. Cooke at the turn of the nineteenth century which appeared in *Off the Beaten Track in Sussex*, 1911.

New Place Farmhouse as it appeared in 1910. Queen Elizabeth I was said to have stayed here in 1591 while on her way from Sutton Place in Surrey to Cowdray. Walter Barttelot Smyth obtained the property in 1774 by an exchange with Lord Selsey who had inherited it from his uncle, Governor Peachey.

New Place was originally part of the Apsley Estate and later owned by Walter Bartlelott. Smyth of Stopham House. The well-proportioned gateway bears on its escutcheon the initials 'I.A. 1569'. The nearby barn was built in the time of Edward I and has lancet windows and stone quoins.

Drawing of New Place by A.S. Cooke as it appeared early in the twentieth century.

The Yeoman's House at Bignor is an outstanding mediaeval hall house dating from the fifteenth century. At the turn of the nineteenth century it served as the village stores and was known as The Old Shop.

Toat Monument was built in memory of Samuel Drinkald in 1823. His father John Drinkald was a Valparaiso merchant who erected the tower close to where his son had been killed after falling from his horse. This view was taken before part of the Stopham Estate was put up for auction at the Pulborough Corn Exchange in July 1911. The original staircase was burnt down in 1938 but has since been replaced.

50

Seven

Lower Street

Lower Street is the principal street in the village. Beginning at the bottom of Church Hill it finished almost one mile away at the foot of Mare Hill. The former smithy (now no. 9) was the workplace of a succession of blacksmiths going back to the seventeenth century. The Child family (father, son, grandson) were working there from before 1782 until after 1852. For the later part of the century it was run by Henry Herrington, after the First World War Frank Crowhurst and finally John Blunden who had ceased shoeing by 1936. The building was sold and used as a garage with a single petrol pump. During the Second World War it was used as a waste paper dump and the premises became very dilapidated before being converted into a bungalow in 1949. This view was taken in 1984 but further extensions were carried out in 1986 so that little of the original building remains.

Templemead was built in 1788 and purchased by a surgeon, Peter Patrick Martin in 1789. It was the home of several doctors and their families until 1936. The photograph here was taken in 1974 when the house was split into two dwellings.

The south side of Templemead viewed in 1982. The Georgian house has a fine curving staircase while the former kitchen and wine cellar were converted into living rooms in the 1970s.

Notice of the auction sale in 1936. An earlier auction of the house contents had been held in 1860, after the death of Dr P.P Martin, when the cellar contained twelve dozen barrels of port and marsala, washing tubs and brewing utensils and in the coach house there was a 'pilentus carriage on patent axles with German shutters'.

The Coach House adjoining Templemead as it appeared in 1964. The ground floor of the former stables had been converted and a boathouse and studio built onto the back of the temple erected by Dr Martin in 1793.

The Sussex Victor Ludorum Cup was won five years running (1958–62) by Lower Street resident and international hurdler P.A.L. Vine.

A child's play house in the grounds of Templemead in 1981. The marble urns came from the gardens of the Crystal Palace after it was destroyed in the fire of 1936.

The seventeenth-century Waterside House was formerly part of the dairy owned by Edward Bowler. The windows were blocked in after the window tax was introduced in 1695. More recently it was the home of Colonel Mullaly and nowadays that of his son Terence Mullaly the art historian.

Timber-framed Willow Cottage dates from the seventeenth century with outside steps leading upstairs. In the 1960s it became an excellent Singhalese restaurant recommended in Raymond Postgate's *Good Food Guide*. At right is the bridle path that formerly led to the eighteenth-century limekiln and to the wooden bridge across the river shown on Richard Budgen's map of Sussex, 1723.

Number 21 Lower Street was built as a Malt House in 1720 with further Victorian additions. The flagstones in the kitchen were laid on an earth floor while the heavy oak beams were 'pinned' with wooden pegs. A cut from the river allowed barges to unload barley and there was a right of way for the master to 'drive a wagon and horses up the lane from the landing stage'.

The barns adjacent to the Malt House were converted into cottages early in the twentieth century and now form one house.

Skeyne House had a very long history before it was rebuilt around 1900 on the site of two old cottages. This view was taken in October 1964 shortly before it was demolished and the land developed to form the housing estate at Skeyne Drive.

Skeyne Drive and the modern blocks of flats (Barclay Court, Belgrave Court and Beverley Court) which were built in the late 1960s.

The approach to the centre of the village in the 1920s. The twin gabled building (at right) was the post office, built in 1906, and which is now a sorting office. Observe the open gutter and the lack of a pavement.

The same view in 1999. The road (A283) has been widened, pavements provided and the wall rebuilt closer to the cottages. However it is not a suitable road for Juggernauts!

The village centre has hardly changed in seventy years. The Sussex Trading Company opened its doors in 1910 to provide groceries, wine, drapery, furniture and ironmongery. By 1980 Cullen's had taken their place and nowadays the store is operated by Alldays.

Looking east up Lower Street soon after the turn of the twentieth century. Oliver Brothers (now Hennings, the wine merchant) is at left and the Arun Hotel at right.

A nineteenth century view of the Arun Hotel which was opened in 1878. Holme Street Dairy is at left of the picture and the adjacent single gable brick building housed the livery stables. Oliver's is at right.

The Arun Hotel was closed and pulled down to provide a terrace of town houses in 1999. Note the change to the façade and the loss of the chimney pots.

A turn of the twentieth-century view of the corner grocery and draper's shop operated by Thomas Cameron who sold out in 1910 to the Sussex Trading Company.

This early nineteenth-century cottage seen in 1893 was to become Killick's bakery at the turn of the century.

Pulborough House was formerly two tiny cottages which were converted to form a bakery, a watchmakers, a dress shop and when this photograph was taken, Dyer insurance agencies.

A pre-First World War view of Stephen Killick's bakery. The bread ovens were at the rear of the premises. The site is now occupied by three maisonettes called *Riverview* and by the Lower Street doctors' surgery, which was transferred from Church House in March 1978.

The opening of the Village Hall by the Duchess of Norfolk on 4 November 1932 was quite an achievement since its cost (£2,220) had to be raised mainly through donations, entertainment and carnivals, although the Carnegie Trust made a grant of £280.

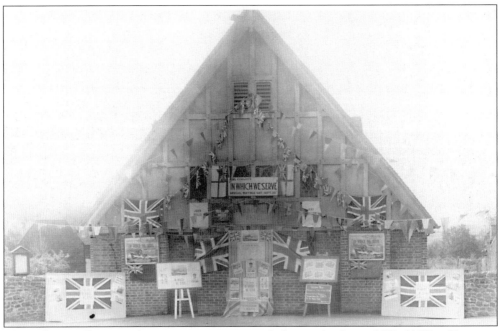

The Village Hall was used as a cinema twice a week during the Second World War. Here it is seen in 1944 promoting the epic film *In Which We Serve* which starred Noel Coward and John Mills. (WSCRO/Garland N 23991)

Wilfred and Mabel Pickles in the Village Hall for the BBC's *Have a Go*, on 22 December 1964.
(Garland Collection)

The village was one of the first in the county to have a public library. Opened in 1926 at the Church Room with a stock of 150 books, it had increased to several thousand by 1939. Both before and during the war years it was run by voluntary helpers, and professional staff were not appointed until 1948. A new library was opened in June 1966, partially rebuilt in 1997, and now has an impressive and useful lending and reference section.

London House was originally two dwellings. In 1903 it became the premises of Oliver Brothers, drapers, grocers and furniture dealers. In her book on Pulborough, Ivy Strudwick vividly describes how the shop was run between the wars and that the shop was so-called because most of the goods for sale had been brought down from London. The property was sold to Mr Tracey in 1945.

London House which is now the premises of Charles Hennings Wine and Spirit merchants.

The Oddfellows Arms was originally a farmhouse built in 1460. Later in the eighteenth century it became a beer house, which it remained until 1960 when a full licence was granted.

To the south of the Oddfellows Arms stands the new village hall which adjoins terraces of new houses on what were, until the 1990s, undulating meadows.

Cecil Strudwick's cycle shop, which was opened before the First World War. It was demolished to make way for the Arun Service Station. This too was rebuilt and became Glovers Garage. It is now vacant and awaiting a tenant.

The east end of Lower Street looking towards Storrington in the 1930s.

These postcards are incorrectly captioned South Street and High Street. The upper card shows Lower Street looking east in the 1930s. The lower card is a similar view taken further east in the 1960s. Pavements are now provided but no motor vehicles are to be seen. However the 'Car Park Opposite' sign no longer applies!

Henleys dates back to the 1600s. Like Waterside House the windows were blanked out to avoid payment of the Window Tax, which was in force from 1695 to 1851. Between 1934 and 1952 the adjacent building, now forming the front of Arundale School, became the Spring Green Lady Guest House which was listed as having nine bedrooms.

Cedar Cottage was known locally as Squib's Cottage before the First World War because the occupier was Mr Squib the local postman.

The junction of Lower Street and Rectory Lane (right) as seen fifty years ago. The large house to the right called The Cedars is late eighteenth-century. In the rear wall of the building are blocked-up arches where once there were doors from which pigs used to be left out to root on Pot Common.

The Red Lion is over 200 years old and seen here around 1890. In 1824 the road was turnpiked and the tollgate was situated at left centre. A drove of cattle had to pay a toll of 10d a score while pigs and sheep were only charged half this price.

The Red Lion Inn looking west, c. 1903.

Eight
Station Road

The Swan Hotel, seen here before the First World War, stood at the junction of the Roman road from Chichester to London with the former turnpike road from Milford to Shoreham. The Swan had eight bedrooms when it became one of the first hotels to be recommended by the AA in 1909. In 1913 it was granted a one star classification which it retained until 1937. Ceasing to be a hotel after the Second World War the building was pulled down in 1959 and rebuilt as a pub and restaurant. This too is due to be demolished in 2002 to make way for houses and flats.

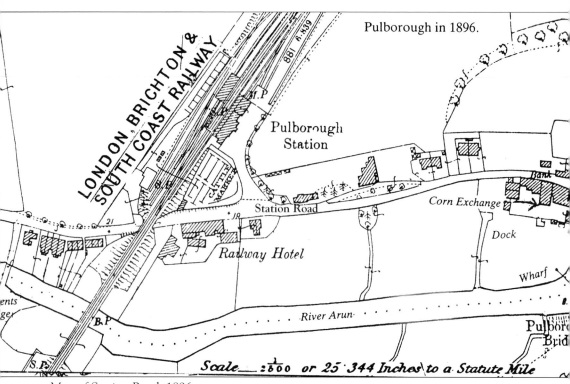

Map of Station Road, 1896.

The Corn Exchange was built in the early nineteenth century adjoining the Swan Hotel and is seen here in 1958 shortly before the building was demolished. The corn market was held every Friday; an annual fair on the Tuesday after Easter for toys and peddlers' wares and a stock market every Monday fortnightly. It was later used as a place of entertainment and film shows were advertised in 1920. During the Second World War whist drives took place in aid of the Red Cross.

WEST SUSSEX

Particulars with Conditions of Sale

of the

VALUABLE FREEHOLD PROPERTY

"FERRYMEAD"

Station Road

PULBOROUGH

In a commanding business position and
with outline planning consent for
development with

SHOP OR OFFICE PREMISES

To be offered for Sale by Auction
(unless previously sold by private treaty)

by Messrs.

NEWLAND TOMPKINS & TAYLOR, F.A.I.

(A. G. Whittaker, F.A.I., D. Scott Pitcher, F.R.I.C.S., F.A.I.,
R. Allden, F.R.I.C.S., F.A.I., P. Bartram, F.A.I.)

On WEDNESDAY, JUNE 21st, 1961
At THE ARUN HOTEL, PULBOROUGH
at 2.30 p.m.

Solicitors: Messrs. Oglethorpe & Anderson, Petworth, Storrington & Billingshurst,
Sussex.
Auctioneers: Messrs. Newland Tompkins & Taylor, F.A.I., Chartered Auctioneers
and Estate Agents, Pulborough and at Petworth, Sussex.
(Phone 300/301)   (Phone 3216)

Notice of the auction of Ferrymead held in June 1961. The name recalled the ferry which existed here in medieval times and probably continued until after Swan Bridge was built.

The two buildings known as Ferrymead were demolished in the early 1960s. These were replaced by a public convenience and three shops with undistinguished shop fronts – one now a ladies hairdresser, another a Chinese restaurant and the third a betting shop. This is an example of how quaint village houses were demolished to make way for the common place.

In 1780 William Harwood built a barn and warehouse opposite the Swan Inn. Used for many years as a corn store, it became a car repair workshop after the First World War, a garage in the 1960s, and a car show room in the 1970s. More recently it has been converted into offices.

Situated next to the Masonic Hall is the National Westminster Bank building which was opened as the Westminster Bank soon after the First World War when this view was taken. Until recently the village boasted three banks but Lloyds has now closed leaving only two.

Motor Bus of the "Sussex Motor Road Car Co. Ltd." and
Managing Director's O

Mr Newland Tompkins, managing director of the Sussex Motor Road Car Company sitting (centre) with Mr St Aubyn on his left. This photograph was taken in 1904 outside Newland Tompkins' Auctioneers' office in Station Road (now Hamilton Cole the electricians). The steam-operated bus ran between Pulborough station and Worthing via Storrington until 1906.

A view of Pulborough as it appeared in the 1950s. Most of the houses visible were on the northern side of Station Road. (WSCCLS)

Fifty years later housing development and blocks of flats have changed the landscape. Now that the water meadows have been infilled the risk of flooding to older properties is much increased.

Station Road in 1906. Until the 1970s water meadows lined the north bank of the river between the Corn Exchange and the Railway Hotel. The railway bridge was built in 1859 by the London and South-Eastern Railway Company when the mid-Sussex line was extended from Horsham to Petworth. The Arun, Prospect and Riverside Court blocks of flats now replace the foliage at left.

The Railway Hotel seen here on market day in 1910. The hotel with its five bedrooms was awarded one star in the AA's handbook in 1927, which it retained until 1942. After the war ten bedrooms were provided and the hotel changed its name to the Pulborough Hotel. It received a two star classification from the AA in 1952, which it held until 1965.

The fortnightly cattle market in progress in 1903. The market continued to be held until the 1950s. The site has since been used as the station car park.

The former Pulborough (Railway) Hotel became the Water's Edge Restaurant in 1966. A small inlet from the river enabled a marina and small boat-launching site to be established but in spite of being recommended for its cuisine by the AA for many years, there was a falling-off in standards, It eventually closed in 1995 and was demolished in 1997.

The high-class riverside housing estate whose ten houses replaced the Water's Edge Restaurant in 1999. The marina and launching site are no more.

The stone-faced railway bridge built over the turnpike road in 1859, now the A283, was adequate for horse-drawn traffic but is both too low and too narrow for the giant transport vehicles which force pedestrians and on-coming traffic to quickly give way.

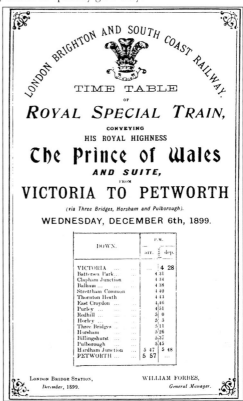

The Royal Train did occasionally pass through Pulborough station. This occurred in 1899 when the Prince of Wales and his suite passed on their way to Petworth House.

Pulborough station entrance before the First World War. The central two-storey block has probably remained unaltered from when the Mid-Sussex Railway opened it in 1859.

Sixty years later the station façade remains little changed. The lamp post has vanished but the goods shed with its canopy remains. (Bowring)

Looking north in 1923, the cattle market is to the right and beyond lies Brewer's brickfield which was in use until 1920. The driveway to the left led to the railway's cattle dock and pens. The platform for the branch line to Midhurst is to the left of the up-line to Victoria. (Middleton Press)

Looking south in 1923, when the present car park area was a goods yard crowded with wagons and traction engines. (Middleton Press)

PULBOROUGH (Sussex)
From Victoria or London Bridge.

Trains from Pulborough.

Leave Pulboro.	Arrive at Lon. B.	Vict.
a.m.		
7 20	9 6	9 16
8 17	9 39	9 33
8 22	9 58	10 13
9 10	—	10 42
9 40e	10 55	10 56
9 42d	11 22	11 7
9 47	11 58	11 57
10 46e	12 38	12 14
10 46d	12 28	12 17
11 3e	1 7	12 43
11 3d	1 2	12 45
11 53	1 31	1 17
p.m.		
1 17	2 56	2 57
2 41	4 13	4 16
3 1	4 50	4 37
5 9	7 10	7 8
6 0	7 45	7 36
8 21	10 7	9 53
8 58	11 11	10 56
10 27	12 36	12 40

Sunday Trains.

a.m.		
7 27	9 33	
8 28	10 02	
p.m.		
4 41	6 35	
5 28	7 32	
6 59	—	
7 17	—	8 53
7 40	9 46	9 47
8 29	10 2	9 53

d Sats. only. e Sats. excepted.

The train service between Pulborough and London was poor until the line was electrified. The 1936 ABC Railway Guide shows there were only two trains to reach Victoria before 10.00 a.m. and the last train from London left at 7.20 p.m. However, electrification in 1938 brought the village within daily commuter reach of the Capital and the service continued to improve until the 1960s when the 6.18 p.m. from Victoria reached Pulborough at 7.20 with only a stop at Horsham. Sadly this service has now deteriorated; in September 2001 the 6.20 p.m. takes 70 minutes and stops at 13 stations.

The fine looking signal box as it appeared in 1923. (Middleton Press)

Clements Bridge, Pulborough. This drawing of the reed-infested river made by Thomas Evershed in 1843 indicates the difficulty barges had in using the river above Pulborough. The house was the local bobby's residence and the tower of Pulborough church can be seen at top left.

The former police station by Clements Bridge. The cells, whose iron barred windows are still visible, overlooked the river.

Clements Bridge, viewed here in 1895, was built around 1793 shortly before the opening of the Rother Navigation in 1795. Its ostensible purpose was to provide access to the meadows for cattle; however, its low arches suggest that its main object was to discourage barges using the toll-free river so that they had to use Hardham Tunnel.

Clements Bridge prior to being repaired in 1923.

However little improvement is noticeable in this 1934 view which shows the line of cottages known as Pinch Plum and the railway signals gantry.

Although token repairs were made from time to time, the bridge seen here in 1966 was eventually swept away by floodwater in the early morning of 16 September 1968. The River Authority removed the ruined piers and used the stone blocks to raise the river wall at Templemead.

Carnival & May Revels

Carnivals in 1931 and 1932 raised £557 toward the cost of building the village hall. A third carnival in 1933 enabled the sum required to pay off outstanding debts to be raised. The Whit Monday carnival programme was supported by fifty-eight local shops and businesses.

Nine
Festivities

The annual carnival was the highlight of the summer. Here the Carnival Queen of 1932 is being drawn by a pair of bedecked carthorses up Lower Street to the village hall.

On carnival day a fete was held in the meadow at the rear of the Oddfellows Arms. This view shows the maypole dancers performing in 1931.

The local branch of the British Red Cross Society was formed during the First World War. The branch patron was for many years Lavinia, Duchess of Norfolk. The Hospital Sunday parade seen here in 1935 raised considerable sums for service and equipment.

The Carnival Queen Miss Sheila Jennings and her attendants on their way to the village hall during the victory celebrations on 10 June 1946. (Garland Collection)

The dedication of the St John's new ambulance by the popular rector the Revd St C.A. (Basil) Maltin, on Sunday 6 May 1973 at the Recreation Ground.

Ivy Strudwick, authoress of *Pulborough – A Pictorial History* (1983), with the flower piece made to commemorate the village hall's silver jubilee in 1957. (Garland Collection)

Pulborough held its first carnival in 1931. Its success can be judged by the welcome it received when the procession approached the village hall.

The crowning of the village's Carnival Queen, Miss Sheila Jennings in June 1946.

The ending of the Second World War and the total defeat of the German and Japanese armies was celebrated on 10 June 1946 by a procession of floats through the village led by the Territorial Band. (Garland Collection)

Before the First World War and until around 1924, the reach above Stopham Bridge was the setting of the annual regatta here seen taking place in 1912. Races were held rowing upstream.

TO ROAD CONTRACTORS & OTHERS.

HARDHAM BROOK CAUSEWAY, NEAR PULBOROUGH, SUSSEX.

TO be LET by TENDER,—The RAISING of the above CAUSEWAY ABOVE the AVE. RAGE LEVEL of the PRESENT ROAD, four feet in height, twenty-four feet in width at the surface, and forty-eight feet at the base, from Hardham Gate to the County Bounds, written Proposals of which must be sent to Mr. Henry Salter, Surveyor. Arundel, before the 8th day of November next, at whose Office a Plan of the Road may be seen, and further particulars known.

            . All letters to be post-paid.

Notice is hereby given.—That a MEETING of the SUBSCRIBERS to Hardham Brook Causeway will be held at the Swan Inn, Pulborough, on Thursday the 8th of November next, at twelve o'clock, to take into consideration the Tenders which shall then be sent in to complete the above Work.

ARUNDEL, *October 25, 1832.*

Hardham Causeway was often subject to flooding in spite of having been raised by 4 ft in 1833 to which this notice in the *Hampshire Telegraph* refers.

Ten
Floods and Storms

Floods often halted river traffic for weeks at a time during the nineteenth century. Even today the causeway between Swan Bridge and Coldwaltham is sometimes flooded after heavy rain. Before the Second World War this was a regular occurrence, which this 1937 photograph shows.

Sunday 15 September 1968 was the night of the Great Flood; it was the highest flood in the Arun Valley in recorded history. This picture was taken on the following morning when the only exit

from the village was through Storrington. The A29, the main road to Bognor Regis was covered up by up to 5 ft of water along Hardham Causeway seen here at the extreme right.

Forge cottages in Lower Street were in deep water in the early morning of 16 September 1968. These fifteenth century homes stood adjacent to the former smithy. Before the Second World War, the cottage on the right was the village bakery. (WSCCLS)

Winters Farm along Hardham Causeway also suffered from the severe flooding in September 1968. (WSCCLS)

A steam train approaches Pulborough station in the 1930s, its reflection caught in the flooded fields of the Arun Valley.

Floods swirling round the back of the Swan Hotel in 1925. (Garland Collection)

A typical view of the flooded river below Pulborough Bridge which would have halted all barge traffic. This photograph taken in 1925 shows the rear of Templemead House. The garden pavilion and boathouse lie between the line of poplars.

Storm damage after the recent November gale. The winds wrought havoc on the village's tallest Italian white poplar tree which stood 200 ft high along the riverbank. This cottage was completely destroyed in 2001 but without loss of life.

Eleven
Southwards to Hardham and Coldwaltham

Beyond the 30mph warning sign on Hardham Causeway is the circular AA yellow sign of Pulborough, erected in the 1930s and denoting its population, location and its distance from London.

Hardham church dates from the twelfth century and contains some of the earliest wall paintings in England. The pictures show the Madonna and the Adoration of the Kings, the Massacre of the Innocents, the Flight into Egypt, Adam and Eve and the Presentation in the Temple.

Old timber-framed cottage in Hardham village, *c.* 1900.

Hardham Priory was a small house of Black Cannons founded by Sir William Dawtrey in the reign of Henry II (1154-1189). It would appear that monks ceased to reside here in the late fifteenth or sixteenth century. This site is now occupied by a farmhouse and only the chapter house has survived. (WSCCLS)

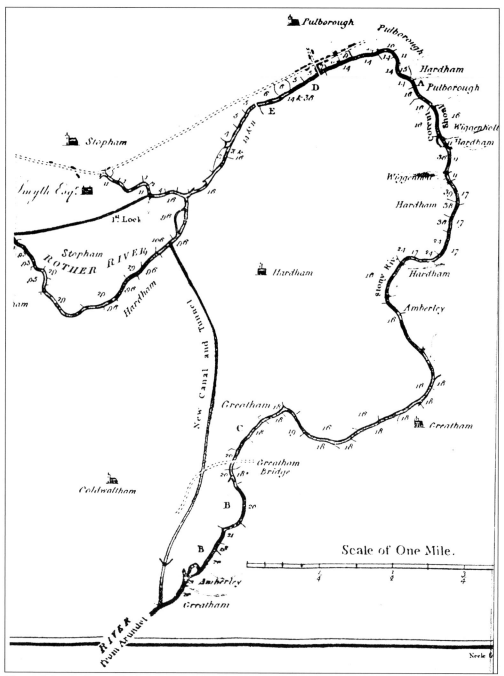

Plan of the Pulborough by-pass canal from Coldwaltham to Stopham via Hardham tunnel, which was opened in 1790. The new cut reduced the distance by $3\frac{1}{2}$ miles but if barges came up with the tide only six hours were saved by using the tunnel. However the toll charge of 9d a ton drove traffic to the old channel except when the river was too shallow or in flood.

The entrance to Coldwaltham Lock in 1908, twenty years after the gates had last been opened to allow barges to avoid navigating the winding river to Stopham via Pulborough.

Coldwaltham Lock in 1933. Part of the lower gate lies forlorn, washed by the incoming tide twice a day. The old lock cottage, used for target practise by the Canadian Army during the Second World War and whose ruins were demolished by the Southern Water Authority in the 1960s, can be seen in the background.

The north end of Hardham Tunnel in 1843. Observe the crude tree trunks used as beams for the lock gates of Tunnel Lock.

The north end of Hardham Tunnel in 1954. The concrete dam was built by the water authority on the site of Tunnel Lock in 1952. The tunnel was blocked beneath the railway lines in 1898. The entrance to the brick underpass for horses, which was built beneath the railway when the Pulborough to Petworth Railway was opened in 1859, was to the left above the tunnel.

The entrance to Hardham Lock in 1941. The lock keeper's cottage was demolished in 1956; the lock and cut were filled in by the river authority in 1968.

Horses towing barges had to cross the River Arun at Stopham by this wooden 'gallows' bridge i.e. a flat beam high above the water with an inclined plane on each side. This 1889 view shows Hardham Mill in the background. The wooden bridge was replaced by an iron structure in 1914.

The cattle bridge across the River Rother above Hardham Mill, 1923. The two red brick piers were oblong in shape and carried black transverse timber beams. There was no parapet. The crossing was used by the Stopham Estate until 1929 and by 1939 only the right hand span remained in situ. (WSCCLS)

The head of water penned by the building of Hardham Lock was later used to operate the corn mill built by George Sharp of Guildford in 1827. In this 1843 drawing the lock-cottage and lock gates can be seen at right. The corn mill was bombed by the Nazis in 1942 and subsequently demolished. The barge at left would probably have come up from Littlehampton to the mill via Pulborough to avoid payment of the tunnel toll of 9d a ton.

Twelve

Eastwards to West Chiltington and Storrington

The approach to West Chiltington church, which is mostly Norman. Note the shingled tower and belfry rising from the great stone roof. The building contains a range of twelfth and thirteenth-century wall paintings of biblical scenes uncovered in 1870. The Norman doorway is admired for its beautiful arch and there is a marble tablet by the altar with the unusual inscription 'Now perjury and forgery can hurt no longer' which refers to a rector of Sullington's wife who died in 1744.

The Great Hall of Nyetimber Manor. Monks from Lewes Priory developed the medieval half-timbered house, recorded in Domesday Book in 1086, as early as the twelfth century. The Manor subsequently passed into the possession of the Goring family, who remained the owners for several centuries. The manor is also well known for its award-winning vineyard which adjoins that of Nutbourne Manor, also celebrated for its white wines.

West Chiltington church, c. 1905.

Storrington as it appeared looking south from Windmill Hill, *c.* 1910. At right is the corn mill which was demolished in the 1970s. The South Downs lie in the background. (WSCCLS)

The main square in Storrington, *c.* 1906. A contemporary bus of the Sussex Motor Road Car Company picks up passengers outside the White Horse Hotel. On the right is Greenfield's Furnishing Store and in the centre, on the corner of Church Street, Greenfield's grocery and drapery shop. (WSCCLS)

Storrington High Street, *c.* 1908. The gas lamp standard was erected to commemorate Queen Victoria's Diamond Jubilee in 1897. At left are the offices of the Capital & Counties Bank and at right Moon's bakery. (WSCCLS).

West Street, Storrington, *c.* 1908. On the extreme right is Mitchell's tobacconist's shop and beyond stands Joyes' bakery and the barn where he stored flour. At left is the Cricketers public house. (WSCCLS)

Thirteen
Westwards to Stopham, Fittleworth and Petworth

Stopham Bridge was built in the fourteenth century, has six small arches and a higher one in the middle raised in 1822 to allow larger barges to pass. This view taken in 1910 shows the old boathouse which was much used at the time of the local regatta. Only its foundations remained after the great flood of 1968 swept it away.

The *Reliance* of Fittleworth moored above Stopham Bridge in 1905 with barge-master Sam Strudwick (holding tiller) and Loyal Saigeman.

Notice in the *Hampshire Telegraph* of 19 December 1831 of the sale by auction of a family residence near Stopham church 'in which is a very convenient pew belonging to the freehold'.

Jubilee Bridge stood between the main entrance to Stopham House and the gate by the lodge. Built by the Bartelott family to commemorate the Diamond Jubilee of Queen Victoria in 1897, it enabled their young children to cross the main road safely. The bridge seen here in 1902 had to be taken down in 1921 when the Southdown bus service between Brighton and Petworth began operation. (WSCCLS)

The entrance to Pallingham Lock as it appeared in 1918. The lock cottage was occupied by a member of the Stone family from 1792 to 1935. The mooring posts are clearly visible as well as the pleasure boat used by Ben Stone, seen wearing his black hat.

The lock house contained in 1911 a living room with cupboard, kitchen, scullery with fireplace, bakery and grocer's shop. Upstairs were three tiny bedrooms, one with a fireplace. On the adjacent wharf were located boarded and brick, pan tiled and slated storerooms, a privy, a fowl house and a small stable. This view taken in 1952 shows the lock keeper's old skiff leaning against the wall. The extensions at each end of the house were remodelled in the late 1930s.

Benjamin Stone, who was lock keeper at Pallingham from 1871 to 1888, seen standing by the footbridge over the lock. As a boy Stone had been a shepherd on the hills and after the closing of the canal had done a fair amount of carpentry including making shepherds' stools. Thurston Hopkins described these home made contrivances as being 'rather in the nature of an up-to-date cane and nickel-plated shooting stick'.

St Mary's church at Stopham is thirteenth century with traces of Saxon work in its walls. A Norman chancel arch encloses the altar and another divides the chancel from the nave. The east window displays six shields of the Bartelott coats-of-arms, the north window was designed by a Flemish artist in the time of Cromwell and the floor is covered with the finest collection of brasses in Sussex.

Stopham Church, Sussex.

Hallelujah Corner, Fittleworth in the 1930s. This accident black spot on the A283 has survived all planned road improvements. The former wheelwright's shop and cottage is at the left of the picture.

Just beyond Hallelujah Corner towards Petworth was the blacksmith's shop. When this photograph was taken in October 1933 horses were still being regularly shod and this work continued throughout the war years. (WSCCLS – Garland)

The Parfoot brothers seen working in the smithy shortly before the furnace was finally drawn in the early 1950s. (WSCCLS – Garland)

Fittleworth Mill in 1899. The mill is best known from the oil painting finished in 1835 by John Constable. However a mill stood to the west of this building in the thirteenth century. In 1615 it was recorded that there was a malt mill and a wheat mill in one timber building close to which, was a rude wharf supported by timber piles.

E.V. Lucas writing in 1904 referred to the Swan at Fittleworth as 'a venerable and rambling building, stretching itself lazily with outspread arms; one of those inns (long may they be preserved from the rebuilders!) in which one stumbles up or down into every room'. The inn with its parlour wainscoted with paintings by artists who once made the Swan their home, has indeed survived and is now a popular hotel and restaurant.

Although the Mid-Sussex Railway from Horsham to Petworth was opened in 1859, Fittleworth did not have its own station until 1889. The branch line was closed for passenger traffic in 1964 and goods trains ceased in 1966. This view was taken in 1896.

Coultershaw Flour Mill, c. 1905. The mill was burnt down in 1923, later rebuilt in ferro-concrete and subsequently demolished. This view is taken from the coal wharf on the north bank of the Rother Navigation; the entrance to the lock is left of the picture.

Petworth House and Lake as it appeared in 1900. The great house is set in the park surrounded by a stone wall ten miles round. Reconstructed by the Duke of Somerset in the seventeenth century it is justly famed for its collection of Turner paintings and the carvings by Grinling Gibbons. Since 1947 it has been managed by the National Trust.

A view of the Market Square, 1910. The handsome market house and court room is built of stone adorned at one end with a bust of William III. It was erected by the 3rd Earl of Egremont in the late eighteenth century.

The reason Petworth does not have a by-pass is not hard to discover. In spite of traffic congestion the choice is between the devil and the deep blue sea. Petworth Park is inviolable unless a tunnel is built beneath it. The alternative easterly route would destroy both the Rectory Meadows (above) and Shimmings Farm (seen at centre below). It is this route which would have been used for Lord Egremont's proposed waterway from Petworth to the Wey Navigation in 1793 but whose estimated cost proved prohibitive so that he chose to support instead the building of the Wey & Arun Junction Canal from Newbridge which was opened in 1816.

Cutting linseed at Strood Farm, Petworth in 1935. The horses are Clydesdales and the machine being used is a converted grass mower. (WSCRO)

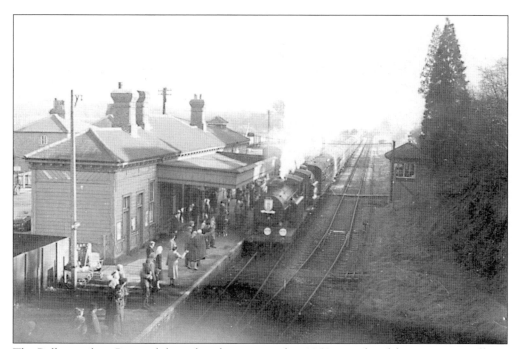

The Pulborough to Petworth branch railway, opened in 1859, was closed for passenger traffic in 1964. This view shows one of the last trains arriving at Petworth station from Pulborough. (WSCRO)

Bibliography

Cooke, A.S. *Off the Beaten Track in Sussex.* (1911)

Cousins, W.L. *Memories of Pulborough.* (1980)

Horsfield, T.W. *The History, Antiquities and Topography.* (1835)

Jerrome, P. and Newdick, J. *Not submitted elsewhere.* (1980)

Masefield, Joan. *Stopham Remembered.* (1991)

Morris, David. (Ed.) *Pulborough before the Great War.* (1986)

Morris, David. (Ed.) *The Pulborough Story.* (1994)

Pulborough Women's Institute. *Pulborough Village in Living Memory.* (1958)

Strudwick, Ivy. *Pulborough, A Pictorial History.* (1983)

Acknowledgements

Many of the illustrations in this book owe their origin to George Garland of Petworth (1900–1978). An enthusiastic photographer he captured not only contemporary events but recorded on camera many scenes of agricultural ways and rustic crafts which have long since disappeared; those showing the blacksmiths shop at Fittleworth are a good example. The Garland Collection is held in the West Sussex Country Record Office (WSCRO)

I am pleased to acknowledge the valuable assistance given to me by Martin Hayes of the West Sussex County Council Library Service at Worthing (WSCCLS) and by David Morris of Pulborough. David has been the editor and writer of a series of books about the village (see bibliography) who was ably assisted by members of a group of local historians who included Elizabeth Garrett, Anne Jenkinson and Richard Leeder. A word of thanks is also due to the many local people in the village who gave me advice and took the trouble to locate old photographs. Although too many to name individually, it would be remiss not to mention Tom Allfrey, Dendy Easton, Guy Leonard, Kim Leslie, Ian Martin, Vic Mitchell (Middleton Press), Terence Mullaly, Fred Saigeman, Christopher and Jane Seagrim, Susan White and Susan Bachelor of Pulborough Library, and the staff of the West Sussex County Record Office. Kay Bowen and Edwina Vine have ably accomplished the task of typing the manuscript and setting out the illustrations.

The Pulborough Society.

Founded in 1972, the Pulborough Society is affiliated to the Council for the Protection of Rural England and the Federation of Sussex Amenities Societies. Its main aims are to make local people aware, through regular newsletters, of environmental problems, planning applications and traffic hazards as well as arranging meetings to which speakers on a wide range of selective subjects are invited. New members are always welcome and should contact the Chairman, Mrs Phyliss James-Crook, Brook Mill, Old Mill Place, Pulborough, RH20 2DR. (Tel: 01798 872124).